Written & photographed by
Wayne Lynch

Whose FEET Are These?

Whitecap Books
Vancouver/Toronto

The information in this book is true and complete to the best of our knowledge. The author and publisher disclaim any liability in connection with the use of this information. For additional information, please contact Whitecap Books, 351 Lynn Avenue, North Vancouver, BC V7J 2C4.

Edited by Elizabeth McLean
Interior design by Warren Clark
Cover design by Peter Cocking and Anne Dunnett
Cover photograph by Wayne Lynch

Printed and bound in Canada

Canadian Cataloguing in Publication Data

Lynch, Wayne.
    Whose feet are these?

    Includes index.
    ISBN 1-55110-860-7

    1. Animals—Identification—Juvenile literature. 2. Foot—Juvenile
literature. I.Title.
QL49.L96 1999   j591.4'7   C99-910259-1

The publisher acknowledges the support of the Canada Council for the Arts and the Cultural Services Branch of the Government of British Columbia for our publishing program. We acknowledge the financial support of the Government of Canada through the Book Industry Development Program for our publishing activities.

Think about all the things you can do with your feet. You can run, jump, dance, kick a beach ball, pedal a bicycle, even balance on a skateboard and do awesome tricks.

Mammals, birds, and reptiles have feet that look very different from yours. Some use their feet to run and hunt, others to dig, climb, or defend themselves. See if you can figure out who owns the feet in this book.

The skin on the bottom of my feet is bumpy like sandpaper. I spend a lot of time in trees, eating the buds, new leaves, twigs, and bark. But tree bark is often wet and slippery. My rough feet help me to grip the branches, so I don't fall and hurt myself.

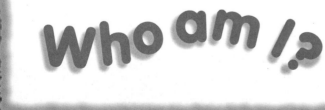

2

3

Some people call me quillpig or pricklepig, but I'm most often called a porcupine. I live in the forests of North America.

Because I am so fat and round, I can't run very fast. To protect myself from coyotes, wolves, and bears, my body is covered with long, sharp needles called quills. If I'm attacked, I swat my enemy with my spiny tail.

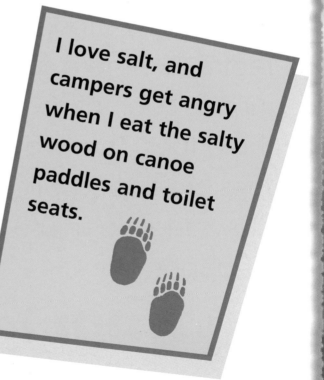

I love salt, and campers get angry when I eat the salty wood on canoe paddles and toilet seats.

I am one of the biggest birds in the world, and weigh as much as a small woman. I cannot fly. Instead, my strong legs and feet make me a speedy runner. Each of my feet has three toes. The two inside toes are tipped with long claws that I can use as weapons.

Who am I?

I am a cassowary. I live in the tropical rain forests of New Guinea, where human head-hunters and cannibals used to live. Even though I can defend myself with my feet, I usually hide when I hear anything coming.

I like to eat ripe fruit, mushrooms, snails, worms, centipedes, insects, and other creepy crawlies that hide under the leaves.

The thick helmet on the top of my head protects me when I race through the forest.

 live in the cold Arctic where it can snow any day of the year. I use the sharp edges on my hoofs to dig through crusty snow to reach the dried grass and other plants I like to eat. My strong horns help me protect myself against hungry wolves and polar bears.

I am a muskox. The Inuit people call me *oomingmak,* the "bearded one." Long hair covers my whole body, and hangs around my legs like a warm shaggy skirt.

In summer, I shed my thick winter coat. Big clumps of wool fall off my body and blow away in the wind. Small birds collect the wool to line their nests and keep their eggs warm.

In the fall, I fight with other male muskox by ramming them with my horns.

My brightly colored feet help me cruise through the ocean. When I dive for food, I steer with my feet. I cannot fly like most birds, but I use my stiff little wings like flippers to fly under-water. I am an expert diver and I can hold my breath for up to six minutes.

Who am I?

14

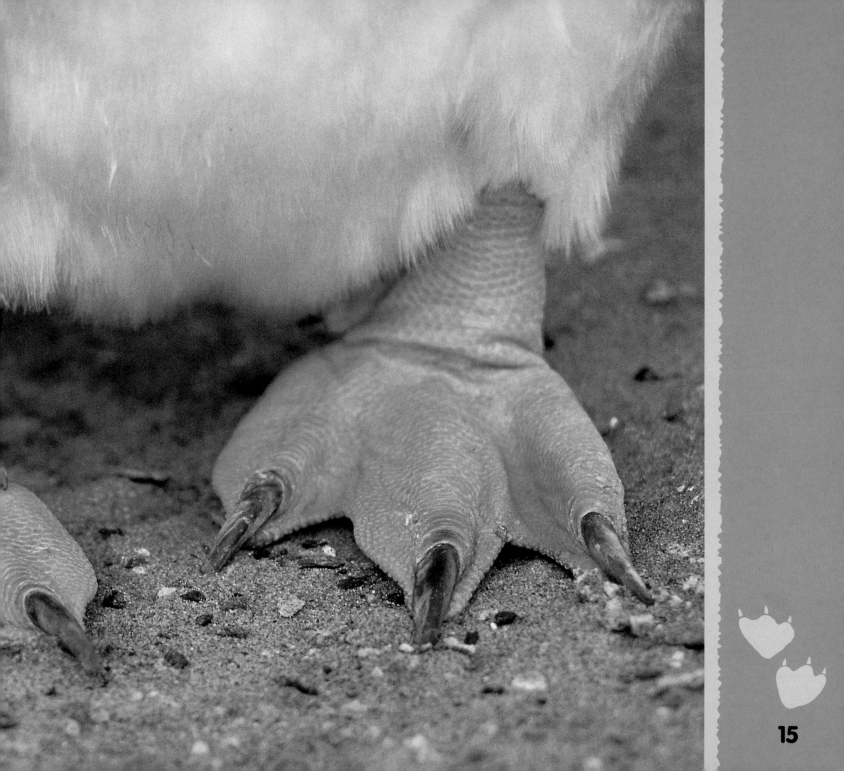

I am a penguin, and I live in Antarctica, the ice-covered continent at the South Pole. Even with my thick coat of feathers, I can still get cold in the icy water. I need lots of food to keep warm.

My favorite foods are squid, fish, and shrimp. During a dive, I can swallow as many as 100 shrimp before coming up for air.

My tongue and the top of my mouth are covered with stiff spines that help me to hold my slippery food.

L ike the rest of my body, my feet are covered by tough scaly skin. I live in the water and swim by sweeping my long powerful tail from side to side. My small feet are only useful when I crawl onto land to warm my body in the sun and digest my meals.

Who am I?

I am a caiman, a close relative of the alligator. I live in the tropical rivers and lakes of South America.

I like to eat fish, especially piranhas, which can't hurt my tough skin. I also eat birds and large snakes. Although I have many sharp teeth, I cannot chew my food with them. I often swallow my meals in one large gulp. Burrr...p.

When food is hard to get, I can live for many months off the fat stored in my long tail.

The claws on my front feet can be as long as a ballpoint pen—longer than any other animal's. I use my claws like a rake to dig up roots or dig out ground squirrels, two of my favorite foods. I also use my claws like a shovel to dig a deep winter den at the base of a tree or clump of bushes.

Who am I?

I am a grizzly bear. I live in the forests of Asia and North America. In fall, I grow fat by stuffing myself on berries and salmon, if I am near their rivers. In winter, when food is scarce, I hibernate.

During hibernation, which is like a long sleep, I never eat or drink. When I wake up in the spring, I am very hungry!

If I were a big male grizzly and if I stood on my hind legs my head would touch your ceiling.

Each winter, I grow thick warm feathers that look almost like fur on my feet and toes, and my toenails grow longer. The feathers work like snowshoes and keep me from sinking when I walk. I need long toenails to scrape through crusty snow, to reach the small seeds and plants I like to eat.

Who am I?

27

 am a ptarmigan (pronounced tar-mi-gen). Even though I look a bit like a wild chicken, I live in the cold Arctic tundra.

In the winter, most of my feathers turn white. This helps me to hide in the snow and protects me from hungry snowy owls, falcons, foxes, and wolves. We live in large flocks in the winter so we can all watch for danger.

On cold winter nights, I often bury myself in soft fluffy snow to sleep out of the wind.

Index